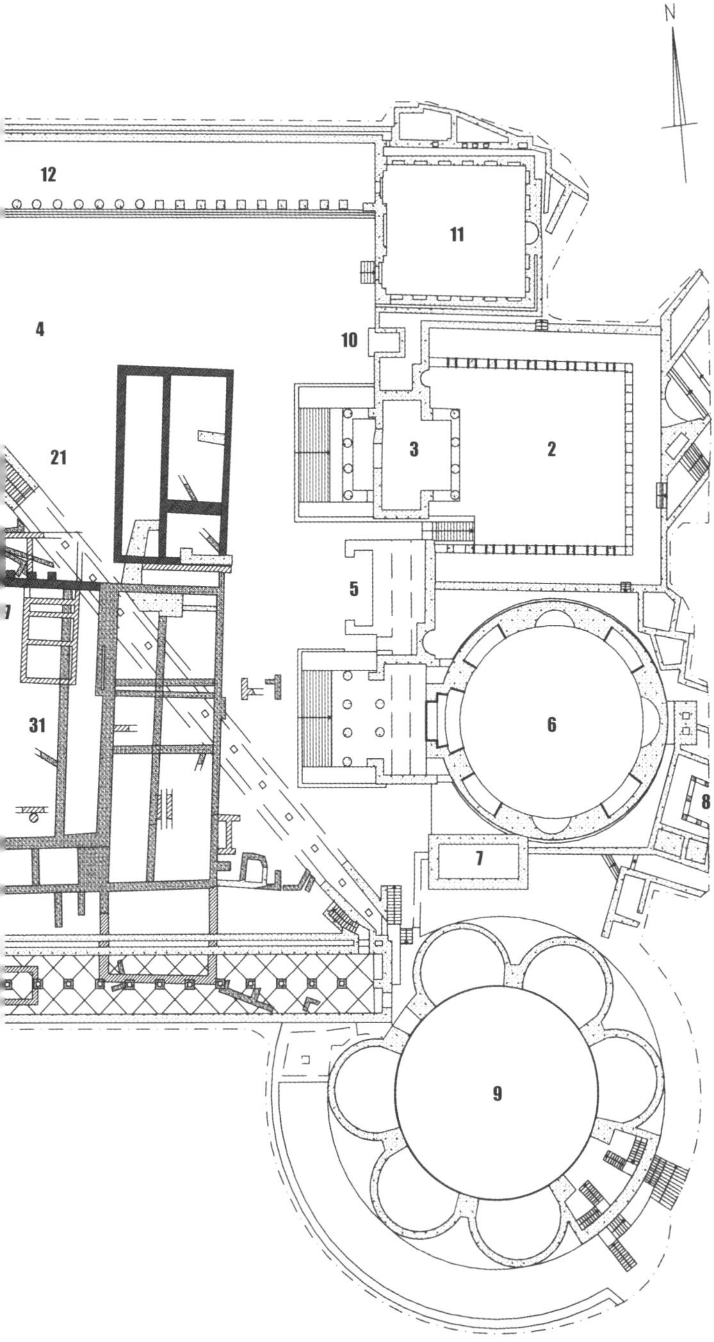
N
12
11
4
10
21
3
2
5
7
31
6
8
7
9

LM Publishers, Volendam, 2016

Tjeerd Dijkstra

Architectural quality

A note on architecture policy

Contents

* The Chief Government Architect of The Netherlands (Rijksbouwmeester) is a private architect who holds that position for about five years on a part-time basis. He advises the Dutch government in the field of architecture and spatial policy. Since 2003 he has been supported by the Colllege of Government Advisors, an advisory group of highly qualified experts in the fields of restoration, landscape and infrastructure.

Preface

What history teaches is how difficult it is to evaluate the products of contemporaries. Necessary renewal is often confronted with ignorance and rejection. This certainly applies to the domain of art and architecture. Only looking back in time, qualities may appear that often were not recognized by contemporaries.
In contrast, the countless selection committees that have to give an opinion on the quality of design, and whose task it is to advise on the choice of an architect, find themselves in a position in which they are expected to look forward in time. The correct judgement must be formed by means of insight and objectivity, that seem to systematically escape objective standards. A seemingly paradoxical position.

This essay by Tjeerd Dijkstra deals with this matter and can be seen as a heroic attempt to create clarity about the question how the quality of contemporary architecture can be assessed. It does this by dissecting the concept of architectural quality in suddenly surprisingly easy to handle parts. What this essay also shows is the responsibility of selection committees and principals to act in the same careful way that is expected from designers. With clear conditions and procedures. With an emphasis on the importance of careful observing and listening.

After its release in 1985 this booklet formed the basis for a new Dutch architecture policy. That even now, after 30 years, it has not lost its relevance, is shown by the publication of this English translation. A whole new target group can take note of it, to which I recommend it warmly. Even with this story, no guarantee can be given that quality in the work of contemporaries will be recognized in time. But it introduces an assessment system in which the correct considerations and arguments are used and where several parties can together come to a balanced judgment.
A designer cannot wish for more.

FLORIS ALKEMADE
Current Chief Government Architect of The Netherlands*

Introduction

In 1985 I was asked in my function as Chief Government Architect of The Netherlands to write a note on the concept of architectural quality. The Chief Government Architect has an important say in the monitoring and assessment of building plans for which the national government acts as client, and there was a need for more clarity about the criteria that were used.

Fifteen years later, in the year 2001, there was a new need for more insight into the concept of architectural quality, this time with Dutch municipalities, that since then were obliged to provide clarity about the criteria they intended to apply for the architectural integration of building plans in their environment. In these documents the concepts that I first formulated in my note of 1985 were often used as general criteria, creating a context for more specific local guidelines.

Today, in 2015, deregulation and decentralization have fundamentally changed the scope of Dutch government's concern with local policies, which means that there is more freedom for the municipalities to decide on these assessment processes. At the same time there has been a spontaneous growth of so-called 'quality teams', consisting of professionals and citizens, whose aim it is to safeguard the spatial qualities of valuable landscapes and city areas in their environment. For those groups too it is important that the discussion about architectural criteria is provided with useful concepts. The assumption that this kind of social concern with the quality of the environment may also exist in other countries gave me a good reason to publish this note again, this time in an English translation.

The 1985 note consisted of two parts: general observations about the aspects that play a role in the development of architectural design, and next to that more concrete information about the procedures for monitoring and assessment that I followed in my function as Chief Government Architect. The first part hardly needed to be updated.

The concepts mentioned in the note of 1985 are of a general nature and are not substantially affected by the changing conditions under which an architectural design is developed. Insofar as they were applicable in 1985, they are still useful today. The second part has been given a wider scope, so that it can be used in different client situations and not only for governmental buildings. This was not a simple operation, as client situations may vary considerably and quality monitoring in architecture and environmental design may be organized in many different ways. Nevertheless, an effort has been made to formulate both a number of basic assumptions and an operational mode with general validity. The reader may judge for himself to what degree this effort has been successful.

TJEERD DIJKSTRA

The difficulty of defining the concept of architectural quality becomes clear if one realizes that in the course of history many successive architectural movements have manifested themselves, often fighting each other with great conviction. Like any other form of human culture, architecture is strongly connected to social development, which is reflected in buildings for individual or collective use. Especially in times of deep social and economic changes that incite cultural reorientation, new movements emerge that reject common concepts and are looking for new avenues. At the same time however, one sees that milestones of architecture, to whatever style period they belong, in the long run become generally recognized, even though it may take some decades or longer before this recognition is a fact. Especially at the birth of new style forms, the ultimate appreciation is often preceded by a period of denial or even absolute rejection. This rejection tends to be more violent as newly developed concepts deviate from familiar images. Many new buildings that later were declared monuments, have at their completion caused violent discussions between supporters and opponents. The more violent these discussions were, the greater the chance that these buildings are recognized, after some time, as monuments of architecture.

If architectural quality, though not always immediately recognized, can be appreciated in the long run, then it should be possible to determine which elements, in spite of all the differences, play a decisive role in its appreciation, so that on that basis one can determine what criteria can be applied. In this note I have tried to indicate and explore a number of those criteria, aspects that play an important role in the evaluation of architectural design.

The following topics will be discussed:

- the relation between form, function and construction
- associative meanings, the language of architecture
- the relation between object and context

- clarity and complexity
- dimensions and proportions
- tools available for the architect to compose with
- restoration and transformation of existing architecture, and
- the way all these aspects are integrated in a coherent architectural concept

The process of evaluation and assessment itself, and the way to incorporate that in the architecture policy of a client's organization is discussed in the last two chapters.

This note does not provide an answer to the question of what is beautiful and what is not. If it contributes to a better understanding and use of the concept of architectural quality, so difficult to grasp, then it will have achieved its goal.

In the course of history many important architects have written treatises about architecture. Vitruvius in the Roman time, Palladio and Alberti in the Italian renaissance, Ledoux, Violet-le-Duc, Morris and Ruskin in the eighteenth and early nineteenth century, and a great number of architects in the twentieth century have tried in treatises, manuals and comments to point out what is crucial in the development of an architectural design. However much their points of view may differ, in all these theories the question is how to compose a building in a culturally relevant way out of material elements in order to meet human needs. The composition of the form is central to the attention, but is always related to the requirements of function (use) and construction (materials).

The lines that a designer puts on paper represent the constructions that together enclose the required spaces and determine the form of the building. Characteristic for the design of an architectural object is that it separates a part of the total unlimited space, which then is wholly or partially enclosed. The effect and usually also the purpose thereof is the appropriation for a special use by individuals or groups: for housing, for performing activities, for keeping valuables, for worship or for restriction of freedom. The architecturally determined space always distinguishes itself from the outside world because it is privatized, appropriated or intended for specific purposes, as opposed to the undefined or otherwise intended outer space. The architectural space is made to fulfil a function. The architectural quality of a space is mainly determined by the degree to which it is suitable for the intended use, even more so if it calls for such use and thus gives it an extra dimension.

In order to determine space, visible matter is necessary, often together with a set of agreements. One can draw a circle in the sand and agree that whoever enters the circle is treading on holy ground. In football matches, the playground is determined by white lines with a special significance that regulates the behaviour of the players. Without these lines, the play would degenerate into chaos. Matter and agreements together determine the usability of the space, which is physically limited and imaginatively determined. The more the limits of the space are materialized, the more architectural the definition becomes. Agreements are gradually replaced by the materiality of the enclosing construction.

This is where architecture is born.

The columns of a temple give a strong architectural definition of the enclosed space. The massive walls of Romanesque churches leave no doubt that it is safer inside than outside. The more the enclosure is materialized and completed, the more it may also have a constructive function: protection against the climate and threats from outside (the separating function) and the bearing of a roof and eventual floors (the bearing function). With the increasing importance of the constructive component in determining the architectural space, the object-character of architecture also increases: the enclosure makes an object of the empty space. The skin gets the character of a material architectural entity with its own compositional aspects, such as size, rhythm, color and texture. Inside and outside are strongly separated and the openings in the walls become of great importance, to allow access and daylight and also with regard to their placement and proportions. Wall openings such as windows and doors gain an architectural significance, breaking through the separation that emerged from the physical need of enclosure.

Art history treatises often associate the concept of architecture with the compositional quality of buildings; in particular with the visual quality of the exterior and the decoration, and, still more specially, with their semantic expression (style, fashion), ignoring that the form of a building is primarily determined by requirements of use and the possibilities to build efficiently with available techniques and materials. Such a sided fixation on style characteristics overlooks the essential connection of architectural form to the requirements of function and construction that together cause its emergence. With its complex effects, architecture transmits the essential content, the intended use and the way that is materially conditioned, to the observer, who will not only find himself outside but also inside the work of art and thus experiences its spatial effects as an active user.

It is notable that especially in periods of architectural renewal, which often coincide with profound social changes, such as for example took place during the industrial revolution, a fundamental reorientation with regard to function and construction gives rise to new spatial concepts and style forms, while in periods of social stability the formal (compositional) aspects get more attention.

Altogether this does not mean that form in architecture would only be a subordinated derivative of function and construction, that it would emerge unmediated therefrom. This last idea was adhered to by early Modernism, but does not stand in thorough examination. On the contrary, just like any language has its own rules with which phrases and texts are built, so the compositional aspect of architecture has its own logic and coherence, which should be known and practiced by architects. The way in which this happens might even be the most determining element of the architect's work, that which defines the 'position', the point of view of the individual designer in architectural culture, that which makes him a recognizable professional. But when the architectural concept as a whole loses the vital connection with function and construction, when architecture is no longer related to these vital components, then the architect becomes a mason without stones, a performer whose acts have become empty gestures. If the public becomes aware of this, it will no longer need his expertise.

Associative meanings, the language of architecture

If forms, that primarily have resulted from functional requirements, available materials and construction possibilities, are frequently and for a longer time used and observed in a particular context, they will get an associative meaning, a life of their own, that may survive, even when the function or the construction of the object has completely changed. Thus the construction of the so-called 'entablature' (architrave, frieze and cornice) in the classic Greek temple is – from a constructive point of view – an illogical translation in stone of the constructions applied in former wooden temples. Pilasters in classical façades refer to pillar structures of temples, without fulfilling the bearing function in the same way. The first automobiles that were produced had the form of a coach including a coachman's buck for the driver, but without horses, simply because the form-concept of a car (automobile = self-moving) had not yet been developed. It took some time before the driver got his now normal place inside the car.

The associative meaning of forms has an important function in architecture because it enables the designer to express what he wants a building to mean for its environment. It also determines to a great extent what people experience when they see and visit a building. In Gothic architecture cathedrals referred to the mystique of the faith. The Palladian villas in Italy refer to the wealth of the owner and the purity of classical architecture, the English garden city refers to the ideal image of the peasant village, the Russian constructivists during the revolution referred in their architecture to the promises of industrialization that would free the world of all conventions, Art Nouveau in Europe referred to the idyllic harmony in nature, and the post-modernists of our time refer to what they feel has been lost with respect to meaningful architecture in the recent period of orthodox functionalism and modernism.

Each style period thus develops new concepts in which it incorporates references and associations with forms that already existed earlier or elsewhere, or that may be expected in the future, in such a way that new attitudes towards life and new expectations can be projected in new associative concepts and thus can be transferred. A new style has more power – and thus more quality – if it is able to offer concepts and forms that are useable as a representation of emerging social values and realities and thus characterize a new cultural period. By the ostentatious refusal to use words from worn languages, the radical DADA movement in the early 20th century tried to make clear that new times had arrived, that needed new words and forms, which indeed were found by the modern movements in art and architecture. The contemporary tendency to just reproduce generally accepted historical forms in a commercial interpretation, instead of being open for a creative renewal of architectural typology, does the opposite and will not contribute to the necessary development of architectural language.

A creative approach of new values and possibilities requires professional sincerity and courage of the architect, for the validity of newly found forms will not be accepted immediately and cannot be determined or proven in an objective way at the moment of their inception. Collegial contacts often are at the origin of new insights and convictions and architectural platforms can do much to stimulate the necessary professional discussion. It is up to the architectural critic to provide structure and depth to the often vigorous public debate they cause, and up to the client to be well informed and careful in the selection of his architect. If these conditions are met the fertile soil is there from which new architectural languages and associative meanings may gradually emerge.

Object and context

As was stated previously, the erection of a building always means a separation, an appropriation of part of the general space for a special, often private use. In this sense there is always a relationship between building and surroundings, between object and context, between individual and environment. If buildings would be conceived as objects that are only concerned with themselves and only have to meet the requirements that come with their intended use, then the town would be composed of a collection of loose elements without any mutual relationship, in an environment that would be no more than an empty space between them; they would be experienced as cakes in a shop-window. Just as a building is a collection of related spaces with a specific use, connected by a system of circulation spaces, so is the city not only a collection of buildings, but also, and primarily, a system of related spaces that have a social function, and serve for circulation and access to the buildings around.

The city space and the space in a building only differ principally in the sense that the city space is public while the architectural space can be appropriated by individuals or specific groups who have acquired the possession or the right of use of the land. In that sense the building is a private object in a public context. At the same time, the public space is defined by the buildings around; their façades and volumes not only determine their own external boundaries but also create the walls of the urban space which they together enclose and define.

Inside buildings there also is a continuous succession from more public to more private, from collective to individual use, ending in the individual housing or working space. A piece of furniture is an object in the context of the building. The separate space finds itself within the context of the building as a whole. The building fulfils, as a more or less recognizable object, a function within the context of the city. So in this way – from chair to city – there is a continuum of mutual determination and interdependency in which recognizable spaces and volumes present themselves alternatively as object or context. The transition from town planning to architecture in this continuum of mutual relationships is located in the boundary between collective (governmental) and private decision power, while in the realm of the latest, an array of nuances between more collective and more private use may occur.

It is of great importance to be well aware of the relation between object and context, because one of the very first quality aspects of architectural design stems from that relationship. Should this just be developed from the intended functions of a building, and should its necessary contribution to the urban context or the surrounding landscape be overlooked, then one of the most important criteria for quality will not be met. This not only applies to an individual building initiative, but also, and to an even greater extent, to building by government authorities, when they acquire sites that are intended for important public functions. Not only should government be the first to serve the interest of local urban quality, it also has the power and thus the responsibility to do so.

That extra complicating factors may emerge as result of the requirements imposed by the urban context on the design of a building, is sometimes felt as annoying. Each experienced designer knows, however, that the tension that results from the necessity to reconcile contradictory internal and external conditions can provide the architectural object with a complex meaning that makes it unique because it transcends the image that would result from its own function alone.

Anyone who realizes how much urban spaces and architectural objects can define and reinforce each other's significance will understand that the contribution to the quality of the urban space is one of the most important criteria for the evaluation of architecture. And not only for buildings in an urban environment or in a landscape does the relationship between object and context play an important role, that relation is also essential for the way spatial elements are part of the building plan itself. The way in which the succession from public to private use of space is given form is the determining factor in the way a building is experienced. The more attention is given, at all scale levels – from chair to city – to the coherence in the varying relationships between object and context, the stronger that quality will be felt.

An important aspect of clarity is that it adds structure to information. Whether it concerns words, sounds or images, the function of structure is to provide support for human observation, to bring order to what is presented to us in time and space in such a way that we can form images that can be kept in our memory. It is not only the primary emotional impression that generates the mental picture of the world around us but first of all the structure in what we can see, feel and hear. What we remember creates the relationship with our surroundings, in the sense that the surroundings become familiar. Both in architecture and town planning, it is clarity with respect to location, proportions, succession and mutual relationships of spaces and volumes, that determines to a large extent which image we will retain. The ring of canals in Amsterdam, the squares and boulevards in Paris, the grid structure and Central Park in Manhattan, they make these cities recognizable for us, they provide them with their own character. Within buildings, it is the structure of the public (circulation) space and its relationship with specific spaces that mainly determines the image that is formed in our mind. If a building is a labyrinth without points of orientation and without accents in the spatial arrangement, then we will experience it as unpleasant and even frightening, because we feel that we might get lost if there is no clarity in the spatial structure. Also in the external appearance of a building, in the proportion and composition of its volumes, in the position and relation of openings in walls, in the division of surfaces and in the use of texture and color, clarity plays an important role: symmetry, rhythm and recognizable measurement systems make it possible to reduce the large amount of visual information that we receive from an architectural object to a comprehensible size, so that we can see and remember a relationship among the constituent parts. To experience a building or an urban environment, the clarity of the 'concept' is of the greatest value.

In a dialectical sense, clarity is the opposite of complexity.

Complexity emerges when different themes come up at the same time within a composition and become related. In the design of a building – as was previously discussed – the environment can cause a spatial solution that cannot be explained from the function of the building itself. Complexity in an architectural composition often is a result of the different influences on the design by functional and environmental requirements. How far and in which way clarity and complexity are united within one concept depends on the attitude and also on the sensibility of the designer. Complexity can serve to respond in a subtle way to contrasting data in the brief of a building and its location, but also as a means to enhance the composition as such. If a design is not only structural and clear but also intriguing and complex, if it does not immediately reveal its coherence, then the observer will be stimulated to discover and try to understand this coherence, and he will be continually confronted with new surprises. Complexity, if understood this way, does not exclude clarity, but is a complementary notion that the designer can use to involve the observer in a more conscious way in experiencing the actual structural coherence. There is a relationship between clarity and complexity like between reason and feeling, between the scientific and the intuitive, between certainty and adventure, between the classical and the romantic, between the formal and the organic, between the Apollonian and the Dionysian..

Clarity and complexity are concepts that in the course of history always return together in human culture but usually as opposing poles, with accents shifting now to one pole and then to the other. This is how human culture continually determines its place between these two poles in the surrounding world. The position taken can often be derived from the way clarity and complexity are treated in architecture. Renaissance architecture can be characterized as a countermove against the religiously loaded architecture of the Gothic, as it resumed the formal themes of the classics in a period in which rational thinking and scientific research replaced the mysticism of the Middle Ages. Also in later periods there is a continuous struggle between architectural movements that endorse a formal objectivity, such as the rational Modernism of the early twentieth century, and movements that seek a connection with the complex subjectivity of an individual emotional experience such as Art Nouveau and the Amsterdam school. Architectural milestones may result when both elements are simultaneously present in a tense relation.

Dimensions and proportions

Architecture has in common with other visual arts that it uses the spatial dimensions of form, size and place as the main elements with which to compose its objects. Together with those, the use of material, texture, color and light plays an important role in the way architectural effects are brought about and experienced. The difference of scale with the other visual arts however, and the fact that the beholder may also be an active user who claims part or all of the architectural entity for his own aims or activities means that the visual impact of those aspects is different.

In the foregoing, the relationship of the form of architectural objects and elements with function, construction and context has been dealt with, as has been done with the aspects clarity, complexity and associative meanings. The degree to which the quality of form is determined by a system of dimensions and proportions has not yet been taken into consideration. Such systems are of essential importance for the quality of a composition. Throughout history and in many cultures, measurement systems have been used to determine the dimensions and the mutual relationship of architectural elements. Sometimes these systems were derived from the sizes and proportions of the human body, sometimes from astronomical or mathematical systems. Often mystic-religious meanings were ascribed to these systems. But why some proportions can count on a general appreciation by many observers, such as for instance the 'golden section', cannot be determined objectively.

That an architectural composition has to have a structure of interconnected proportions is understandable when one realizes that human observation rests on the determination of analogies and differences and that an image in which no order has been brought can only be absorbed with great difficulty. But why the proportions of one space or object are more pleasant than those of another, why some proportions in the design of a façade are more balanced or exciting than others, can hardly be determined, even though it appears that different persons – especially those with an experienced eye – often come to the same appreciation. Insight in the effects of measurements and proportions cannot be based on theoretical grounds, but only reached through empiricism; it appears from experience that some proportions are good, but not why.

This observation implies that one of the most important characteristics of the quality of an architectural composition is the hardest to catch in a clear definition and therefore also remains the least testable. After the discussion of the relation of architectural quality with function and construction, object and context, clarity, complexity and associative meanings, we remain speechless before that which is in fact the essence of a composition: the proportions. There is only one way to learn to master their qualitative aspects: look around and study them consciously, and for the architecture student, learn by designing and exchanging experiences with others. In that way the evaluation of proportions will get an intersubjective, and thus more general character. However, which proportions are good or bad will never be determined objectively.

Architectural tools

What remains are the tools with which the abstract design on paper is transferred into physical reality: materials, texture, color and light. At the present state of technology, the possibilities in the application of those tools are practically endless. This in contrast to previous cultural epochs in which the technical possibilities were more limited and the construction of buildings had to be done with a restricted amount of available local materials and traditional craftsmanship. The consequence was a greater natural unity in the architectural appearance, which moreover was strongly locally bound. However great the advantages of the present freedom of choice and of the highly developed technical knowledge may be, they tend to create, exactly because of the lack of restrictions with respect to available materials and techniques, an incoherent image. It is therefore important that the choice of material, texture and color and the use of light derives its meaning from the architectural composition. If materials are chosen apart from the context of the architectural design, if they are applied on the basis of their decorative effect without fulfilling a function in the coherence of the total concept, then they will only damage its quality. Profusion caused by excess makes the image incoherent and unclear. So by restricting his choices the designer should use the means in such a way that they have a maximum impact and remain subordinate to the spatial coherences that are intended in the architecture. This does not mean that profusion is always misplaced, but it becomes uninteresting and loses its intriguing effect if it does not have control and discipline as its polar opposites.

In the end, light is the key to architectural experience. Visual observation ends where there is no light. Light, whether it is daylight or artificial light, does not only enable the activities for which a space is meant, it also makes the nature and the boundaries of a space tangible, and in so doing contributes to an important extent to the atmosphere in which the activities take place. Just as the light in a painting comes from the pallet of the painter, so the light in a building comes from the drawing table of the architect, well balanced and in the right areas so that it enhances the spatial experience. Light fills the gap between physical reality and human observation. It is the task of the architect to combine natural light and artificial lighting in such a way that they not only enable the intended use of the building, but also, and even primarily, stimulate the perception of space by its users and visitors.

Restoration and transformation of existing architecture

Monitoring architectural quality as described previously does not only apply to new buildings but also to restorations or transformations, however small or large they may be. There will be a shift of accents but not of a completely different approach. The difference between restoration and the design process for a new building in an existing situation is often not more than a matter of scale: in a restoration or transformation the existing building acts as the context for the new design and special attention will be given to associative meanings because the result will have to tell the stories of both the original and the new state.

Throughout history two main approaches can be seen in the practice of restoration: the approach that tries to repair its object in such a way that a supposed original state is as much as possible brought back, and the approach in which only what is left of the original state is conserved, and new elements are added that, while carefully in balance with the architecture of the existing building, show clearly in what time they were designed and realized. It is clear that this last approach allows more freedom to add new life to old buildings and to reuse them for new purposes, thereby preserving and often even strengthening their cultural significance.

In this note the different aspects that play a role in the assessment of architectural quality have been discussed separately. The quality of an architectural design as a whole depends not only on how the designer has dealt with each of these issues, but also, and essentially in the extent to which the design process as a whole has led to an inspired concept that brings the different aspects together. In addition to that it is of the greatest importance that the design is carefully worked out and detailed. This should be done by, or under the supervision of the architect, who should be involved in the building process as the representative of the client so that he can oversee and control in detail the correct realization of the project.

Design processes and the assessment of architectural quality

The design of buildings is a complex iterative process with a great number of feedback loops, in several phases, in a number of mutually related areas and on different levels of detailing. The designers look for solutions that provide a coherent and optimal answer to the given design problem.

Like in a soccer game, the delineation of the playing field and clear game rules form the conditions that stimulate the creativity of the players. A maximum of clarity from the principal at the start of the process with regard to requirements and procedures and a minimum of disturbing interventions during the process form the conditions under which a team of designers, consisting of the architect and his consultants, will come to integral and optimal solutions. To ensure that they feel full personal and collective responsibility for the result of their efforts, the criteria for the assessment of the design should be formulated as clearly as possible prior to the beginning of the design process, so that once that has started the designers have as much freedom as possible. Monitoring architectural design in a process like this should be done at a certain distance, but without losing contact, and being available for the design team to discuss and answer questions that may (and will) arise during the design process, and to which the brief gives no answer.

In the assessment of a design, two different kinds of criteria may be distinguished: quality criteria and cost criteria. Cost criteria can be formulated in a quantitative way and can be treated objectively. At the start of a design process a preliminary budget should be established according to the brief and the given situation. In the course of the process and in consultation with architect and consultants, this budget will be specified within the different design disciplines (construction, services, landscaping, etc.) and should be definitively established when the final design is approved. The assessing is done by reviewing the calculations that are produced by the architect and his consultants during the several phases of the design process. It should be done on a professional level and is primarily the responsibility of the client, using the available knowledge inside or outside his organization. If the cost calculations that come with the design are not within the limits of the budget, then the architect will provide an explanation for that and – if required – will offer the client possibilities for alternatives that can solve this problem. If these alternatives are not available or not acceptable to the client, then either the budget or the requirements, or both, have to be adapted. In a well phased design process such problems should be addressed at an early stage. If they appear too late in the process, when already too much time and money have been invested, the design process may come to an end without a result, or the client will be forced to spend more money than intended. In a well-organized design process this unpleasant result can and should be prevented by all concerned.

The quality criteria are described to a great extent in the brief of the project: what spaces are required for which activities, what requirements arise from these activities, both regarding the spaces themselves and their mutual relationships; what are the requirements to the construction, the climate, the lighting, the acoustics, the maintenance, etc. Insofar as these requirements are not specific for the building concerned, they can be found in existing norms and regulations.

The monitoring of a design in progress with regard to all requirements will be done continuously by the design team during the whole process and by the client when the architect reports to him about the progress of the plans. As much as possible, the requirements and criteria must be objectively and quantitatively formulated.

Because criteria for architectural quality can only be described in general terms, it is important that the architect keeps his client well informed about the considerations that emerge from his growing insight in the design problem, explaining the deeper understanding of the specific aspects of the project that emerge during the design process. This is important, because it can lead to necessary changes in the brief that otherwise would not become clear in time.

In the circular research process of the design, the monitoring by the client should to a certain degree follow the designer, in order to avoid that the assessment of the architectural quality has a frustrating or even quality degrading effect at the end. Monitoring a design process asks from the client that he is a critically involved, but also detached listener in order to allow for the development of a coherent concept by the architect and his team. The subjective character of the criteria means that a careful assessment of a plan will in a sense always be interactive. It takes place during the exchange of thoughts between the designer and the reviewer during the design process. The architectural assessment does not only regard the design itself as an answer to the specific design problem, but also, and sometimes even primarily, in its relationship to the environment.

The functional and financial requirements that the client and the architect agree upon at the start of a design process can and should be used as hard criteria, in all phases of the design process. This does not go for architectural quality, which asks for a more detached, and, where possible, stimulating approach, that is different in the several phases of the process. These phases are:

- the analysis of the brief in relation to the environmental and site conditions
- the development of the architectural concept (preliminary design)
- the elaboration of the architectural concept (final design)

In the first phase close attention should be given to the interpretation of the brief in the environmental context. For renovations and restorations, the historical and architectural values of the existing building are an important part of that context. If at this stage there is no clarity about the starting points and conditions of the project between client and architect, then this will cause problems in later stages.

At the stage of development of the architectural concept, the initiative lies entirely with the designer. Too much personal interference by the client will disturb the design process at the expense of quality. The client acts as a critical listener and tries to understand the line of thought of the designer. He asks questions and delivers his comments, the discussion being about what is important for, in particular, the inner consistency of the design in relation to the requirements and the starting points. Aspects of architectural quality will be discussed in this context. Monitoring at this stage takes place by checking whether attention has been given to all relevant aspects and whether the design as a whole is sufficiently consistent. If in the view of the client one of the requirements is not, or not sufficiently met, then the design process is carried on until a satisfactory result has been achieved.

At the stage of elaboration of the concept the greatest problems will have been solved. The contact between client and architect remains intact and the design at that stage will still be improved and enriched. The client maintains his task as a critical commentator: a sounding board for the architect, directing his attention to details that had escaped his attention or for which he had not yet found a proper solution. If a process develops in this way, the final assessment is a formality.

Monitoring by the government

Since 1901 the Dutch Housing Act (Woningwet) has obliged municipalities to control the architectural integration of building plans in their environment. This tradition was based on a typically Dutch cultural phenomenon: public awareness of the importance of a well-kept urban and natural environment for the survival and well-being of communities continuously menaced by the aggressive powers of the surrounding nature.

In this process of assessment of architectural quality, the concepts that were formulated in this note have, since its publication in 1985, often been used as general criteria, creating a context for more specific local guidelines.

Today, in the year 2015, deregulation and decentralization have profoundly changed the scope of Dutch government concern with local policies, which means that there is more freedom for the municipalities to decide upon these monitoring processes. At the same time, there has been a spontaneous growth of so called 'Quality Teams', installed by local or regional government, and consisting of professionals and citizens, whose task it is to promote and safeguard the spatial qualities of valuable landscapes and city areas in their neighbourhood. Also for these groups it is important that the discussion about architectural criteria is provided with useful concepts. The assumption that this kind of social concern with the quality of the environment may also exist or grow in other countries was the main reason for publishing this note in an English version.

For any kind of quality monitoring by government of spatial development or building plans, there are some principles that are important to hold on to.

First of all, monitoring should be based on an evaluation of the history and the morphology of the existing environment to which a new building or transformation project is meant to be an addition. This evaluation, based on broad and professional research, should be of a general nature, with the specifications that are needed to make it applicable to the actual project.

Second, the government should respect the monitoring aims and be willing to cooperate in realizing them, first of all by commissioning the design to a team that may be expected to work with the necessary professionalism and to understand and meet the criteria for architectural quality in their designs.

Third, the actual monitoring should be done by qualified professionals, and should start with a discussion with the client and the designers about the way the new development can be a contribution to the existing context, so that the plans that will be developed have a reasonable chance to be approved in the end.

Fourth, the monitoring should follow the lines as described above, based on clear starting points and leading to an inspiring creative process in which problems are identified and solved in time.

Monuments of architecture and otherwise valuable historical buildings or urban ensembles deserve special attention. The necessity to reconcile the requirements of new use, that gives new vitality, with the preservation of historical values, requires extra concern by those who are involved. Because these values often transcend local interest, regional or national government should monitor and facilitate these processes on the proper professional level and with the necessary professional assistance. An official service within the monitoring organization should have the task of documenting these buildings and ensembles on the basis of careful research and to assist private clients and their architects. In this way the necessary intensive guidance, sometimes in detail, can be given without causing delay in the development process.

Choice of architects, architecture policy

If one realizes that architectural quality has to be delivered by an architect and cannot be forced in a monitoring process, then the consequence is that the choice of an architect should be done with the utmost care, on the basis of a number of criteria.

The architect and his office must be able to design and realize the project in a technical and organizational sense. With starting offices, shortcomings in this respect can if necessary be compensated for by collaboration with a more experienced colleague or with a technical consultant. What never can be compensated for is the capacity to design in a professional way, which involves the capacity to analyze the design problem, and develop an architectural concept that meets the requirements of the client in accordance with the cultural values in the urban or rural environment. Here the choice of an architect becomes a matter of policy.

For this reason, both in private organizations and in the public realm, decisions about the choice of an architect should be taken at the board level, and cannot be left to technical services. Of course the officials who are charged within the client's organization with the preparations for the concerned building project must be consulted about this choice. In addition, advice from independent architectural experts who can judge the significance of the commission in the right perspective can be of great value. A competition among architects can, if so desired, open the opportunity to weigh several alternatives for solution of the design problem and to involve those who are concerned with the project inside or outside the client's organization. However, after a careful and, where needed, broad orientation, the decision about the choice of the architect has to be made by those who are responsible at the highest level for the policy of the organization.

In the determination of the final choice, it is important that candidates indicate with which consultants they intend to collaborate. This is even more important in cases in which the consultant has the task of supporting a young architect with little experience. Architect and consultants must be able to work as a team in solving technical and organizational problems. Above all, there should be certitude about a strong personal commitment of the chosen designers to the design problem. If this commitment involves a critical attitude – also towards the client – this should not be seen as a disadvantage. On the contrary, if a strong and independent view on the design problem is the result of that commitment, it may not be qualified as arrogant and should have a full chance to contribute to careful decision making.

By following these principles, clients can play an important role in stimulating good architecture and give opportunities to new talent. In particular, bigger professional clients, having wide experience and expertise in their organization, are in a position to give opportunities to promising young architects, who often have difficulties in developing their professional practice, caused by a lack of experience and contacts.

Though specialization in, or special experience with some sectors of projects may seem to the client to be a guarantee of a professional approach to the design task, it also has its disadvantages, particularly in the case of projects that are not so specific that they ask for such specialization. The advantages of an open-minded and intelligent approach to a new problem by a less experienced but talented designer should always be weighed against the disadvantages of a possibly less inspired routine handling by a specialized office.

The question whether local architects should be called upon for projects in the region needs a nuanced answer. On the one hand it is clear that for small projects in particular, familiarity with local culture can be an advantage. On the other hand a certain distance from local interests is desirable and the criterion of architectural quality should never be questioned. In practice it should be recommended in the case of modest projects to appoint local architects, as far as that is possible without making concessions to the quality criterion. The larger or more specific a project is, the greater the chance that offices outside the region will have to be called upon.

The competition as a means to arrive at the choice of an architect asks for a nuanced approach. The disadvantages of competitions are the lack of proper contact with the architect during the development of the architectural concept and the large quantity of lost work that is done by the architects who are not chosen. On the other hand, in special situations, the competition among capable designers of a different signature can have its advantages for the client. Also, public procurement, in which the competition on architectural quality is an important element, is obligatory for large projects under European rules.*

An important question that has not yet been answered is how the principal can make his choice of an architect in the tricky field of different architectural trends. In the previous discussion about the associative meanings of an architectural image, it has been pointed out that especially with regard to this aspect there is a relationship with several architectural movements. When dealing with the question of how this should affect the architecture policy of the government, it is important to realize that these movements follow each other quickly, sometimes in a just a few years. Therefore it would be dangerous and could be disruptive in the development of contemporary architecture if authorities would limit themselves to just one movement and give no opportunities to others. If we accept the assumption in the first chapter of this note – and there is a reasonable consensus about this within the architectural community – that architectural quality can be appreciated separately from architectural movements that endorse specific ideas and theories, then the obvious conclusion is that government authorities should not limit themselves to one

* More about the way competitions and public procurement are organised the Netherlands can be found in publications by Architectuur Lokaal, an independent knowledge center in the field of Architecture in Amsterdam (http://arch-lokaal.nl).

movement only, and should test whatever new movements come along on the basis of quality.

For a private client, the situation is different. One may, and even must expect from him, that with the choices he makes he takes sides, and in so doing gives direction to the development of architecture. In the course of history, the private clients in particular were often the ones who ensured that new movements got opportunities. Their motive was often not primarily the expression of their own preferences or taste, but more a general interest in the development of architecture and a strong involvement with new cultural developments. Nowadays there seem only few individuals left who want to, and can fulfil a role as patron of the arts. So the more important it is that companies and organizations that do have this ambition assume their role. In the end, what is at stake in the development of architecture policy is the authentic dedication to architectural quality in a society that appears to be increasingly dominated by short-term economic values.

Colophon

Text
Tjeerd Dijkstra, Edam

Book design
Piet Gerards Ontwerpers, Amsterdam

Printed by
Dekkers Van Gerwen, Dordrecht

Binded by
Boekbinderij Hoogendijk bv

ISBN 978 94 6022 423 2

LM Publishers, Volendam
info@lmpublishers.nl
www.lmpublishers.nl